The engagement of Prince Henry and Lady Alice Montagu-Douglas-Scott confirmed that romance had blossomed at last between the shy soldier Prince and the beautiful daughter of the Duke of Buccleuch. Theirs was to be a happy partnership, based on a shared love of the outdoors and a strong sense of duty. But fate dealt them a cruel double blow.

BEGINNINGS

WHILE PRINCE HENRY WAS BEING GROOMED FOR A LIFE
OF ROYAL RESPONSIBILITY AND PUBLIC SERVICE, ALICE
WAS ENJOYING A PAMPERED AND CAREFREE CHILDHOOD

ON 31 MARCH 1900, AT YORK COTTAGE, THE Duchess of York, later to become Queen Mary, gave birth to her fourth child. She was delighted. 'I confess I am just a little bit proud of myself for having produced another boy which was greatly wished as alas we have so few princes in our family,' she wrote to her Aunt Augusta, the Grand Duchess of Mecklenburg-Strelitz. She ended over-optimistically, 'I now I think have done my duty and may now stop, as having babies is highly distasteful to me tho' when once they are there they are very nice! The children are so pleased with the baby who they think flew in at my

Right Prince Henry at the age of one, looking adorable in the stiff white petticoats worn by all Edwardian babies. The young Prince had been christened in the Queen's Private Chapel at Windsor below. The ailing Queen Victoria named him after various members of the Royal Family, and her daughter Beatrice composed a special hymn for her new godson. Other godparents included Kaiser William of Germany and Field Marshall Earl Roberts, a hero of the Boer War

window & had to have his wings cut off!'

The new Prince was christened Henry William Frederick Albert in the private chapel at Windsor on 17 May 1900. After the ceremony, old and failing Queen Victoria recorded that 'the baby was brought into the chapel after the 1st Hymn (by my dearest Albert) and wore the old historical robe which was first made and worn by Vicky.' She also noted that he was 'a

Hulton Picture Company

proper school – not least because they would have a chance of mixing with other boys. The Prince of Wales would not hear of it, however. No princes so close to the throne had ever gone to school.

In 1907 David left for the Royal Navy College at Dartmouth and Harry joined Bertie in the class-room. He quickly showed the same ungovernable temper as his brothers when confronted with subjects he found difficult. His uncertain health did not make things easier. He had one severe cold after another, and in February 1909 was laid up with a 'slight attack of influenza' which affected the base of one lung. By March, however, Harry had recovered. When his father asked him what he wanted for his ninth birthday, he responded eagerly, 'I should like a small model of an aeroplane, if it is suitable. I had thought of a fly-book. Also a box with a spring for letters.'

Sent to Broadstairs

But Harry's sickly constitution continued to cause concern. At the age of ten he was sent to York Gate House, Broadstairs, the residence of one of the Royal doctors, where Sister Edith Ward kept an eye on both his health and his education. Here the little boy began to write regular letters to each of his parents, a practice he was to continue until their deaths. 'Dear Papa,' he wrote the day after his arrival. 'Broadstairs is a very nice place and I like being here very much.

very pretty little boy'.

Prince Henry was a generally placid infant. As he grew into toddlerhood, however, he began to display the explosive and volatile temper characteristic of most of his family. As a fierce little two-year-old, he responded to his Aunt Augusta's request for a kiss by sharply slapping her proffered cheek.

Highly strung and delicate

Harry, as his family called him, was an under-sized and delicate child. Like his brother, Bertie, he had knock-knees and had to suffer wearing splints. The highly strung brothers had tempers that were not improved by having to submit to this painful ordeal. Albert developed a pronounced and mortifying stammer. Harry had frequent outbursts of crying and, later, uncontrollable giggling fits. He was also intimidated by his two boisterous older brothers. Bertie and David, the future King George VI and King Edward VIII, often fought furiously and some bullying of a younger and more vulnerable brother was inevitable. Fond though his parents were, there was no question of any of the children running to them with their woes. The stern Prince of Wales believed in a firm hand. His mother, gentle though she was, was unable to comfort her offspring with hugs and kisses. Harry eventually confided his fear of his brothers to a sympathetic governess, 'They worry me,' he told her forlornly, 'They worry me.'

Tuition of the Princes was mainly entrusted to former schoolmaster Mr Henry Peter Hansell. In the mock class-room at York Cottage he applied himself to the task of preparing the two older Princes for the Navy. They proved as hard to teach as they were to discipline and their academic progress was dismal. Hansell was of the opinion that they would benefit by attending a

♛ *Henry spent his childhood at York Cottage on the Sandringham Estate above. It was a happy home, but all the Duke of York's children had to endure a rather stern regime and the frequent absence of their parents when they were away on foreign tours. At such times, their grandparents, nanny and tutor made sure that a strict eye was kept on behaviour*

> ## 'I confess I am just a little proud of myself for having produced another boy...'
>
> THE DUCHESS OF YORK

♛ *Prince Henry stands to attention with a miniature rifle, in a pose that anticipates his adult career in the army right. But despite his boyish bravado, the Prince was a delicate child, and his parents felt much anxiety about his weak legs and susceptibility to infection*

Hulton Picture Company

The house is very near the old Fishermen's Pier where the life-boat is launched. I have half finished the dog puzzle which I am trying to do.'

This change of scene, however, did not stop him still being miserable when he has to do his lessons. 'I am glad you spoke to him about the sudden fits of crying,' his mother wrote to Sister Edith after he had been there for about ten days, 'for tho' I feel he sometimes cannot help it, yet he ought to be gently cured of this tiresome nervous habit.'

The young schoolboy

Like Hansell, Sister Edith believed that the Prince's nerves would benefit from mixing with other boys at a proper school. And the Prince of Wales, who by now was impatient for his son to learn to 'behave like a boy', finally agreed. In a historic decision it was decided that Harry would attend St Peter's Court, the local preparatory school. Arrangements were being finalized when, on Friday 6 May 1910, Edward VII died and the Prince of Wales became King George V. 'I am so awfully sorry that dear Grandpapa is dead,' Harry wrote to his father, 'and that you Mamma, Grannie and Aunt Toria are in such trouble. I shall try to help you by being a good boy.'

And try he did. In fact, Harry took to school life better than anyone had expected. He did not throw temper tantrums and his headmaster

👑 *Prince Henry with his father at Balmoral in 1906 left, the year that he began his education in the York Cottage classroom. At the age of ten he was sent away to school and, to his family's surprise, he adapted very well to his new life. As a scholar at Eton above he was highly popular and enjoyed mathematics and rowing*

Hulton Picture Company

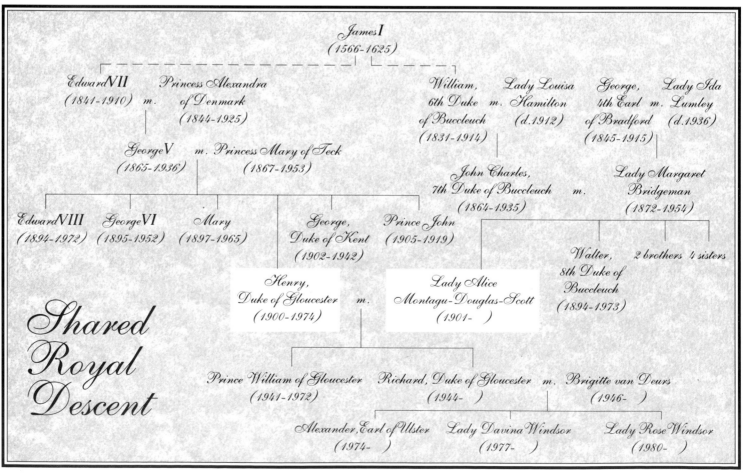

Shared Royal Descent

James I
(1566–1625)

Edward VII   Princess Alexandra
(1841–1910)   m.   of Denmark
                         (1844–1925)

William,   Lady Louisa   George,   Lady Ida
6th Duke   m.   Hamilton   4th Earl   m.   Lumley
of Buccleuch   (d.1912)   of Bradford   (d.1936)
(1831–1914)   (1845–1915)

George V   m.   Princess Mary of Teck
(1865–1936)   (1867–1953)

John Charles,   Lady Margaret
7th Duke of Buccleuch   m.   Bridgeman
(1864–1935)   (1872–1954)

Edward VIII   George VI   Mary   George,   Prince John
(1894–1972)   (1895–1952)   (1897–1965)   Duke of Kent   (1905–1919)
                              (1902–1942)

Walter,   2 brothers   4 sisters
8th Duke of
Buccleuch
(1894–1973)

Henry,   Lady Alice
Duke of Gloucester   m.   Montagu–Douglas–Scott
(1900–1974)   (1901–   )

Prince William of Gloucester   Richard, Duke of Gloucester   m.   Brigitte van Deurs
(1941–1972)   (1944–   )   (1946–   )

Alexander, Earl of Ulster   Lady Davina Windsor   Lady Rose Windsor
(1974–   )   (1977–   )   (1980–   )

longer undersized. On 16 July he obtained a commission as a second lieutenant.

'Gentleman Cadet Henry, HRH Prince' left Sandhurst with an assessment of 'above average' ability. However, it was felt that the Prince would benefit from a futher period of study, and he was sent to Trinity College, Cambridge, to do a short course in constitutional history, economics and French in October 1919. On 30 July 1920, his education now complete, he joined the 13th Hussars at Warburg Barracks, Aldershot.

The Royal Hussar

The young Prince took to the life of a subaltern in the Cavalry as a duck to water. He was conscientious and well liked by all the ranks. Two years later he was transferred to the 10th Royal Hussars, a regiment which he came to regard as his own. It was here he became close friends with Lord William Scott, brother of the woman who would one day become his wife.

In many ways, Alice Montagu-Douglas-Scott was born into a way of life even more opulent than that of the Royal Family she was to join.

♛**Above** *Baby Alice sits on her mother's knee surrounded by her older brothers and sisters. On the left is Walter, William is at the top, Sybil cuddles her mother and Margaret Ida sits on the right. Mary, Angela and George have not yet been born*

reported that there had been 'no cause to complain of his behaviour towards anybody'. Although his academic performance was poor, he did his best. He also learned to play cricket, though he complained that he never made any runs – possibly due to the fact he was still having to wear splints and special boots. By the Christmas term he even managed to top his form in arithmetic and proudly carried off the prize at the end of the year.

From St Peter's Court Harry went to Eton, where he was known as 'Henry Windsor'. Although his scholastic record was less than brilliant, he had met the challenge of being the first King's son ever to attend the school. Many years later a prep school contemporary recalled him being 'well liked by everyone' because he was 'ordinary & had a sense of fun'. This attitude was to serve him well at Eton. He was cheerful, modest, good fun and, like all new boys, did his stint of fagging.

First taste of army life

In 1914 World War 1 broke out and Harry busied himself knitting comforters for the troops in the trenches. He also joined Eton's Officers Training Corps. This experience confirmed his determination to join the Army. He sat the entrance examination to Sandhurst in March 1918 and in May received his formal acceptance. He was almost 18 and, at 5'9", no

MYSTERIOUS HAUNTINGS

Visiting Drumlanrig before her marriage, Alice's mother nearly fainted when a furry shape suddenly appeared in a candlelit corridor. She was even more terrified when, years later, a huge monkey materialized on a chair. During World War 1, when Drumlanrig served as a hospital, a matron fled after being awoken by 'something awful'. It was subsequently revealed that the room she occupied was called the Yellow Monkey or Haunted Room.

Alice also saw a ghost at Drumlanrig while ill with diphtheria. 'A little girl in a long frock came to talk with me,' she recalls. 'No doubt I was delirious, but it would not surprise me if she really was the ghost of some child who had lived in that room generations before'

Third daughter of the immensely wealthy seventh Duke of Buccleuch, she made her appearance on Christmas Day 1901. The birth took place in her mother's corner bedroom at Montagu House, the Buccleuch's residence in London's Whitehall. Long since demolished, the house sheltered behind tall trees roughly opposite the gateway into Horse Guards Parade. The large garden, with its sweeping lawn, immaculate flower-beds and old Chinese pagoda, ran down to the Embankment and the air echoed to the hoots of ships and barges on the busy Thames. Liveried footmen were on hand to open the front door and answer bells. A magnificent white marble staircase led from the entrance hall to the vast reception rooms and a warren of bedrooms on the upper floors. Despite this grandeur, however, Alice recalls only one bathroom in the entire building. 'I can't remember who was allowed to use it!' she said years later.

Garden games

The garden provided the most fun for Alice and her seven siblings. A favourite game was to hang over the wall overlooking the Embankment and dangle wire spiders on elastic strings in the path of pedestrians below. Another thrill was being allowed to watch her grandmother, who was Mistress of the Robes to Queen Alexandra, setting off for a court function in the Buccleuch state coach. This magnificent vehicle had silver harnesses for the horses and the family coat of arms picked out in twinkling fairy lights. The little Scotts also attended Queen Alexandra's annual children's party. On one occasion a troupe of naked pygmies performed a tribal dance. Alice and her sister Sybil were so taken by this that for several weeks afterwards they pranced about without any clothes on when they should have been tucked up in bed.

John Frost Historical Newspapers

♔Above *Alice's equestrian training started when she was very young: the three-year-old horsewoman was strapped into a special seat on her pony 'Vixen'*

♔*Montagu House, the Scott family's London residence below, was chiefly occupied during the summer months. It was an imposing house with plenty of space for the extended family of eight children and their parents, aunts, uncles, cousins, grandparents and scores of servants and nannies*

In such a large family the Scott children were inclined to pair off. Sybil was Alice's inseparable companion – except, that is, when Lord William (Billy) returned for the holidays and Alice was abandoned for his older and more sophisticated company. Like others of their class they were taught at home and, being exuberant, they had a high turnover of governesses. Mary, Alice's younger sister, had the worst temper. On one occasion the little minx actually tried to push one poor teacher – an immensely tall woman named Miss Maffey – out of a window!

Seasonal moves

The Buccleuchs' life followed a seasonal pattern, as they moved from one house to another. Each of their six houses had its allotted place in the calendar. The family normally spent June and July in Montagu House in London, so that Alice's father could attend the House of Lords and watch the cricket. The scale of wealth was such that when the family went to the annual Eton and Harrow cricket match at Lords, they took lunch for 150 people. The kitchen maids were up at four hacking at ice blocks to produce the necessary hundredweight of ice chips to preserve the food for the journey. Yet although London was fun, the Scott children felt they belonged in Scotland, and were thrilled when in July the family left Montagu House and took the train to Eildon Hall in the Scottish Border country. They could scarcely wait for the moment when the train stopped near Penrith to fill up with water and Nanny opened the window to let them breath in the first scent of the moors.

From Eildon they moved on to join their

Hulton Picture Company

'Very shy and rather plump, I made a miserable début at a dance at Windsor'

ALICE

ALICE'S PLEDGE

When she was 14, Alice and her sister Mary were taken to Seascale on the Cumberland coast. Alice dashed into the sea. A short while later, overtaken by a giant wave, she was floundering out of her depth. 'Wherever I searched with my toes for the bottom there was a frightening void. I began to feel too tired to go on: "I'll drown and be done with it," I thought.' Luckily she came to her senses. 'Oh God, give me my life,' she prayed. 'I promise I'll make use of it if you give it back to me.' A moment later she found her feet touching rocks and was able to scramble back to safety.

She was to honour her pledge many years later, when marriage gave her the opportunity to dedicate her life to public service

Derek Forss

paternal grandparents at Drumlanrig. Seen from a distance this pink granite castle soars above the surrounding countryside like a fairy-tale vision. Here Alice and Sybil spent magical hours galloping their ponies along the miles of grass rides that wind through the woods and along the river bank. In the afternoons they fought mock duels under the ancient yew trees or watched sea-trout leaping the waterfall. Another favourite pastime was hide-and-seek which, with Drumlanrig's four towers, endless long passages and plenty of dark cupboards and secluded nooks, was particularly exciting. Christmas was spent at Dalkeith, near Edinburgh, or at Bowhill in the Scottish Borders, and the family usually visited Boughton House in Northamptonshire in the spring.

When Alice was 12 and Sybil 15, they were sent to a boarding school at West Malvern in Worcestershire. If nothing else it made them more appreciative of home, 'the joy of the holidays amply compensating for all the boredom of the long and seemingly endless terms'. At 18 Sybil got married and Alice left to spend several months at a Paris finishing school. On her return she was immediately plunged into the dizzy world of coming-out dances. Shy and rather plump, she made her début at Princess Mary's birthday ball at Windsor. Hiding behind a column in a too-tight white satin frock, she was too miserable to notice that 'Prince Henry was ill at the time and had to miss the occasion'. Romance for Alice was still to come.

☙ *One of the great attractions of Boughton, where the family spent Easter and early summer, was the motorbike with a wicker side-car owned by one of the cousins who lived on the estate. As a special treat, Sybil was allowed to ride it round the grounds, and Alice accompanied her as a passenger* below

John Frost Historical Newspapers

Softly draped
neckline

Deep cuffs of
fox dyed the
colour of
chinchilla

The gown is pulled in at
the waist with a deep
sash decorated with
a spray of violets

The flowing lines
of the dress echo
the draped styles
of ancient Greece

Lynne Robinson

♛Frivolous hats gave a much-needed fillip to the
formal styles of the 'thirties and 'forties,
especially after clothes rationing came in. Alice
wears a simple straw-brimmed hat enlivened
with flowers *below* and a very
fashionable little number perched
on the front of the head,
complete with veil
bottom

♛ *Left* Norman Hartnell designed not only the wedding dress
but also a number of outfits in Alice's trousseau. He was soon
to become the Royal Family's favourite dress designer – a
position he kept for over 40 years. This evening-dress made of
velvet is supremely elegant and yet would also have kept Alice
warm on the chilly evenings of her November honeymoon

FIT FOR A DUCHESS

Alice's concern with fashion was thrust upon her when she became Duchess of Gloucester. Public interest in Royal clothes was as avid in the 'thirties as it is today, and numerous magazine and newpaper articles seized the opportunity to dissect the fashion style of this new member of the British Royal Family

♛ *Below* Made of heavy satin coloured a very pale pink, Alice's wedding-dress was cut on the bias so that it closely followed the line of her figure. An unusual arrangement of orange blossom decorates the simple neckline. The waist is defined by a wide sash and the skirt flares into a long train that gradually narrows to a point. A bridal crown of tiny pearls, orange blossom and silver filigree holds the long tulle veil in place

THE SPORTING LIFE

WHILE PRINCE HENRY PURSUED A MILITARY CAREER AND BEGAN TO TAKE ON MORE ROYAL RESPONSIBILITIES, ALICE SPENT MUCH TIME IN HER BELOVED AFRICA, ENJOYING HER FREEDOM

P RINCE HENRY, ONCE SUCH A SICKLY CHILD, was now a vigorous young man with a passion for sport. He played as often as he could and was undeterred by physical danger. In February 1921, for example, the horse he was riding fell into a ditch, trapping Harry underneath. Writing to his father, he casually reported that, struggling up, the animal 'caught the top of my head with the toe of his hind foot and cut it rather deep'. School had also taught him cricket, rugby, tennis and football, and as a Cavalry officer he took to hunting with gusto. While at Sandhurst he also asked his father for permission to take up boxing. Despite the fact that a fellow cadet had died after a particularly savage match, it was given readily. The King considered it 'a most manly sport, thoroughly British & teaches you to keep your temper'.

A difficult position

By 1921 Harry's military career was causing the King and his advisers anxiety. One problem was that Harry was approaching his 21st birthday and would soon be required to undertake a variety of Royal duties. Another, more important, concerned the nature and locations of military exercises considered appropriate for a King's son to engage in. Despite deploring the violent actions of the Sinn Fein, King George had already decreed that Harry could not take up arms against his Irish subjects. Now he also decided that he was not to take part in any of his regiment's strike-breaking activities. With unemployment in Britain exceeding the one million mark, strikes and protest marches were being staged all over the country. Public order was increasingly a military concern and this veto put Harry in a difficult position. Both factors prevented him gaining the experience necessary to a Cavalry officer and significantly curtailed the normal development of his career.

Banned from accompanying his regiment on a posting to Ireland, Harry first became a temporary ADC (personal assistant) to Lord Cavan, then helped Bertie – now Duke of York – with his public duties. When his regiment returned in March 1922 he was finally able to rejoin them in Canterbury. Pleased though he was, Harry found his routine duties as commander of the Third Troop of C Squadron tediously dull. He was a man who needed constant challenges and compensated for lack of excitement with sport. He went point-to-pointing, played polo and shot whenever he could. 'I was most lucky on Thursday in getting 4 woodcock the first two being a right & left,' he wrote to his father. The King was suitably impressed: woodcock rise late and fly so low that to hit one at all requires great skill. 'Getting a right and left woodcock,' he wrote approvingly, 'is not often done.'

In January 1923, Prince Henry embarked on a six-month course to perfect his horsemanship. It was not, however, to be a good year for him. In February he fell during an equestrian exercise and twisted his ankle. A few weeks later he injured the same ankle again when his horse shied and crushed his leg against a wall. At the beginning of March a car in which he was travelling collided with a lorry and overturned. Two weeks later he fell and hit his head during another riding exercise and suffered concussion. This was followed by a long bout of flu and he was still suffering the after-effects when Bertie married Lady Elizabeth Bowes Lyon in April. But there was more. In August he was schooling a horse when the horse slipped and fell on his foot. The result was a plaster cast and a couple of months spent hobbling around on crutches.

State duties

In June 1924 the King and Queen of Rumania visited Britain. Harry was at the King's side to welcome them and attended all the grand functions held in their honour. Pleased with his performance, his father asked him to fulfil the same role when the King of Italy made a state

The professional soldier of the Royal Family, Prince Henry was posted into the 10th Royal Hussars in 1921. He was promoted to captain in 1929, then to major in 1934; he hoped eventually to take command of the regiment. In the photo above, Henry sports the regiment's cap badge in the form of the Prince of Wales's feathers

visit a few weeks later. These were Prince Henry's first important state duties and an introduction to the increasingly prominent position he would have to assume. It was not until November 1926, however, when he attended the marriage of Crown Prince Leopold of Belgium to Princess Astrid of Sweden, that he represented the King abroad. But in March 1928 the King created Henry Duke of Gloucester, Earl of Ulster and Baron Culloden.

On safari

Although Harry's desire to accompany his regiment on postings abroad was consistently opposed, he was nevertheless to experience plenty of foreign travel in the years to come. In September 1928, he set off for a safari holiday in Kenya. The party was after big game but Harry had decided not to shoot more than two of any species unless more meat was needed.

In 1929 Prince Henry made his debut as a Royal ambassador on the world stage of international diplomacy. His first mission was to Japan where, with the object of furthering good relations between the countries, he conferred the Order of the Garter on Emperor Hirohito. His arrival on 2 May was greeted with a loud volley of

All photos: Hulton Picture Company

👑 *The Prince of Wales (third from left) lines up for a photo call with his younger brother Henry (second from left) and other members of the Royal Family on his return from his Indian tour of 1922 left. Without much in common, Henry and David were not the closest of brothers. But although Henry did not display much feeling when his brother told him he planned to abdicate, David sensed his disappointment*

👑 *Horses were one of the Prince's first loves. Above He is shown taking a fence in his regiment's point-to-point cup race at Ashridge Farm, Wokingham, Surrey. Henry was to win the race*

👑 *As time went on, Henry took over a greater number of Royal duties from his two older brothers. One of these was attending the Agricultural Show at Leicester in July 1924 below*

ILN Picture Library

Hulton Picture Company

EARLY ROMANCE

Beryl Markham was a stunning married woman when she met Henry on a Leicestershire hunt. In 1928 she helped arrange living conditions for Henry's East African safari, and the two began to spend time together. The story that he was the father of her son, born in 1929, has been disproved, but that she was his mistress for a short time seems certain. She went on to become the first woman pilot ever to fly from England to America

gun salutes, and children waving Japanese and British flags lined the route into the capital. 'On Friday morning,' he wrote to the King, 'we had the Investiture which was a very impressive ceremony, & luckily none of us made a mistake…I found it very difficult walking backwards when wearing the mantle!' But in 1941, when Henry was told of the Japanese attack on Pearl Harbor, he exclaimed, 'And to think they made me travel 10,000 miles to give the Garter to that damned Mikado.' Harry went to Ethiopia the following year for the Coronation of Emperor Haile Selassie. Here, too, he performed his part with dignity, investing the 'King of Kings' with the Grand Cross of the Royal Victorian Order.

Harry's problem of combining military life and Royal obligations was not his parents' only concern. On his return from his 1934 Australian tour, the question of marriage – first broached a few months earlier – was brought up again. 'Mama & I have always been anxious that you should marry and settle down,' his father wrote, '& I am sure you could find someone who would make you a good wife & be a help to you in your duties.' Perhaps the King and Queen were not aware that, some years before, Harry had already met and admired the woman who was to be his wife.

A country girl

Like her future husband, Alice loved sports and all aspects of country life. During the early 1920s she indulged her special passion for hunting as often as three times a week. When winter weather conditions prohibited a meet, there were paper-chases through the woods or fast, furious and competitive games of ice hockey. On one occasion she and her friends challenged some Hussars at their barracks. It was a hard-

☙Above *Henry visiting the Yasukuni shrine in Japan, where he laid a wreath. The Prince was awarded Japan's highest order, the Grand Order of the Chrysanthemum, during this 1929 trip, which he found interesting but exhausting. More to his liking was a big-game hunting expedition in East Africa the previous year* below right. *His bag included two buffalo, a lioness, a record-breaking oryx cow, an impala and an eland*

fought match and resulted in one girl breaking her ankle. A penchant for practical jokes was another thing Alice and Harry had in common. These ranged from harmless pranks like apple-pie beds to stitching mustard plasters inside the seat of pompous young men's evening trousers and watching them suffer through dinner.

A beloved continent

In April 1924 Alice accompanied her sister, Sybil, who was recuperating from influenza, to Algeria. It was her first encounter with the continent that would ever after occupy a special place in her heart. Two years later she visited Africa again. This time she went to the Cape, where her elder sister, Mida, was marrying the ADC to the Governor-General. She was taken on many sight-seeing tours, including one to the awe-inspiring Victoria Falls. For Alice, however, the unrivalled highlight of the whole trip was a rugged safari in Zululand. The party took no tents, and a minimum of equipment was carried on a single wagon. The itinerary included a rhino shoot, but Alice was told it was too perilous for her to join. Consequently, when the men set off at the crack of dawn she was left behind with some of the African helpers. They were busy tidying up the camp when she glanced around to discover that

Hulton Picture Company

the Africans had disappeared and were cowering under the wagon. The reason quickly became apparent: trotting calmly towards her was a mother rhinocerous and her baby calf. Quick as a flash Alice dived under a camp bed where she lay quaking and praying until the danger had passed. Ironically, when the hunters returned later they were empty-handed and had not seen one rhino the whole day!

Unfortunately Alice's South African idyll ended with an attack of cerebal malaria. On the train journey home, while crossing the equator, she developed a raging fever and became delirious. For several terrifying hours she thought she was a tree planted in a sealed tin. It seemed to her that, as her branches grew outwards they were bent and bowed by the confined space. Her great good fortune was that a Dr Rabaliate, the most respected authority on tropical diseases, also happened to be on the train. His prompt intervention – and medicine provided by one of the other passengers – saved her life.

Despite this frightening experience, Africa's unique magic had captured her affections. Back

Hulton Picture Company

♛ *'Crossing the line' aboard the HMS* Sussex, *1934* left. *This elaborate shaving ritual takes place upon crossing the equator for the first time*

'Mama & I have always been anxious that you should marry and settle down'

GEORGE V TO HENRY

in England, and despite her hunting, Alice was restless and unsettled. Feeling an increasing need to make herself useful, she offered her services to the Selkirk Red Cross. In 1929 her uncle Francis Scott, who had settled in Kenya, brought his young family over on a visit. Before leaving he invited Alice to come over to stay with them. Tempted though she was, her father was showing the first signs of the cancer that would eventually kill him and she was reluctant to leave him. This dilemma was resolved while she was

♛ *By the time she reached her mid-20s, Alice had turned into a stunning young woman who had many suitors but no desire to marry yet* below

Hulton Picture Company

Edinburgh Photographic Library

pondering the problem during a long solitary walk. Suddenly a deer appeared, jumped over a fence in front of her and galloped away. 'There' she said to herself. 'That's an omen. I must get up and gallop away too.'

Alice was to live at Deloraine, her uncle's farm, for more than a year. The two-story building was presided over by the formidable Miss Loder who acted as housekeeper, nanny, cook and dairymaid. Alice's own servant, Kimani, also served in turns as maid, driver, bodyguard and general factotum. She paid him sixpence a day, which covered his food and living expenses.

⚜ *Bowhill, near the River Tweed in the Scottish Borders* above, *was one of the many Buccleuch family residences, and the one most associated with the writer Sir Walter Scott, a relative, who refers to it in a poem as 'sweet Bowhill'*

⚜ Below *In 1926 Alice accompanied her eldest sister Margaret (Mida) to Cape Town, South Africa, where she was to be married to Commander Geoffrey Hawkins*

Her aunt and uncle were often away, and on those occasions she was left with the ultimate responsibility for the day-to-day running of the farm. She travelled widely, met many colourful characters and made many friends. 'I have never been happier,' she was to say later, 'and look back on this episode in my life as the greatest possible piece of good fortune.'

It was in Kenya that Alice began to experiment with water-colours to record what she saw. She was pleased with her efforts so, returning for a second six-month visit in December 1931, she took plenty of art materials with her. Back in

'I have never been happier'

ALICE ON HER TIME IN KENYA

Together they motored hundreds of miles exploring the country in Alice's Citroën. She saw giraffe, ostrich, wildebeest, lions, tigers, leopards, zebra and antelope in their natural habitat. Often nervous families of screeching monkeys would streak in front of the car. These forays were not without risk, however. Even the main roads were only packed mud which became impassable after heavy rains. Bridges too were a rarity – often consisting of no more than a couple of planks – and an electrical storm upstream could suddenly transform a dry river bed into treacherous torrent.

In Kenya Alice enjoyed the freedom of being able to do and wear pretty much what she liked.

Hulton Picture Company

DELORAINE

In 1920 Alice's uncle, Lord Francis Scott, embarked upon a new life, farming in Kenya. He chose a plot of land situated not far from Nairobi and started organizing the building of the house, to be named Deloraine after a hill near the family estate in Selkirkshire. Together with his wife, two small children and a governess, the family endured the primitive conditions of three mud huts while work was in progress. Alice's Aunt Eileen, who had lived a life of great luxury as daughter of the Viceroy of India, did her best to recreate the environment to which she was accustomed. Deloraine was splendidly furnished, family pictures hung on the walls and, every night, the dinner table sparkled with silver. Eileen also designed the pretty flower gardens with their brilliant shrubs, and the kitchen gardens in which she grew many English vegetables

England the old restlessness resurfaced and in the autumn of 1933 she was ready to leave again. Her father, however, was getting thoroughly impatient with all the to-ing and fro-ing. He was not, he said, going to give her any more money, and if she wanted to go to Africa again, she would have to pay all the expenses herself.

To help raise the amount she needed Alice held an exhibition of her Kenyan paintings at Walker's Galleries in London's New Bond Street. It was a gratifying success and far exceeded her

⚜ *The Earl and Countess of Athlone at Brantridge Park, their Sussex home* above. *The Countess was first cousin once removed to Henry, and as a child and young man he saw much of them, while Alice's sister Mida was lady-in-waiting to the Countess. In 1935 the couple invited both Henry and Alice to visit them for Ascot*

expectations. An encouraging review in *The Times* read, 'In Africa the artist seems to have risen to the occasion and, with imagination stimulated by unusual shapes and colours, produced a series of records which are interesting pictorially as well as from the topographical point of view.' To her delight she sold most of her pictures, making 190 much-needed guineas.

A fateful letter

Back at Deloraine Alice resumed her now-familiar Kenyan routine. She helped on the farm, visited friends, painted and went on many safaris. She was happy, carefree and thoroughly enjoyed life. In 1934 she decided to visit her youngest brother, George, who was stationed at Lucknow in India. Booking a return ticket, she boarded ship for Bombay. One of the most exciting moments of her trip was her visit to the Khyber Pass. To get there it was necessary to go through 'tribal territory' where women were not allowed, so she and her companions dressed up as men in big Afghan coats.

Then, in the spring of 1935, the Duke's health took a worrying turn for the worse and she was promptly summoned home. She had scarcely shaken the dust from her shoes when a letter arrived from Princess Alice and the Earl of Athlone inviting her to stay at their beautiful home, Brantridge Park. Little did Alice know, when she accepted the invitation, that a matchmaking plot was under way and that another very special guest had been invited too.

Camera Press

Hulton Picture Company

ILN Picture Library

👑 *Above left* Alice's delicate tiara, earrings, bow brooches and the lower of her two necklaces all come from Queen Mary's wedding gift of a turquoise and diamond parure. The necklace consists of 26 clusters of turquoises and diamonds, matching the earrings and ring. The brooches had been a confirmation gift to Mary's mother, who gave them to Mary at her wedding

👑 *Far left* Alice on her way to Westminster Abbey in the robes of Extra Dame Grand Cross for the installation of the Knights Grand Cross

👑 Major HRH the Duke of Gloucester *above*. Prince Henry was married in the magnificently braided full-dress uniform of a Major of the 10th Hussars

STATE REGALIA

GLORIOUS ARRAY

Prince Henry's position as a Duke gave him ample scope to indulge his love of ceremonial dress, while Alice made a dazzling Duchess resplendent in the many wedding gifts from her mother-in-law. 'Don't buy a lot of jewellery in a hurry,' Queen Mary had written to her son, 'because...I have various ornaments which I have long ago selected for your wife from my collection'

☙Another of Queen Mary's wedding gifts to Alice was an emerald, pearl and diamond suite, some pieces from which are pictured *above*. The two bracelets are actually not a pair but Alice has always worn them together

☙*Left* At the Coronation of King George VI, Prince Henry wore the full regalia of a Royal Duke. He was officially created Duke of Gloucester on 30 March 1928. The title had been held, as the King wrote to him, 'by members of our family for many years'. Previous holders were Thomas Woodstock, son of Edward II, created in 1385; Humphrey Lancaster, son of Henry IV, created in 1414; Richard Plantagenet, son of Richard, Duke of York, created in 1461; and, for a short period before the Battle of Bosworth Field, Richard III. He was followed by Prince Henry, son of Charles I, in 1640 and Prince William, son of Frederick Prince of Wales, eldest son of George II, created in 1764. The only Duke of Gloucester ever to make it to the throne was the infamous Richard III and, because of this, there were those who considered the title an inauspicious choice and wished the King had chosen another for his second son

Hulton Picture Company

DESTINED TO MARRY

ALICE AND HENRY WERE FRIENDS FOR MANY YEARS. BOTH KNEW INSTINCTIVELY THAT, WHEN THE TIME CAME TO THINK OF MARRIAGE, FRIENDSHIP WOULD TURN INTO LOVE

W HILE IN ALGERIA IN 1924, ALICE AND HER sister took a trip to Biskra, an oasis town in the Sahara desert. It was not only the exotic atmosphere that struck her, but a bizarre encounter with an old man who told her fortune by drawing marks in the sand. After pondering the signs long and hard, he told her that her destiny was to be a special one and she would marry a person of considerably higher station than herself. To Alice this sounded like amusing nonsense – after all, she was already a Duke's daughter. The old soothsayer, however, was insistent: 'I see a

crown and much to do with an army. You will travel greatly, many long distances.'

Prince Henry was not privileged with such a tantalizing glimpse into his romantic future. He met the beautiful young Alice through her brother, who was one of Harry's truest and most trusted friends and a fellow officer. Lord William – Billy to his family – had served as a soldier in World War 1 and earned himself the Military Cross for distinction and gallantry. Harry was still shy and insecure. He very much admired Billy's war record and his greater experience of life. Their shared fondness for night-life and having a good time was also an important ingredient in their friendship.

In 1922 Harry rejoined his regiment, now at Canterbury. Being an officer in a regiment at rest, however, was not much of a challenge and he

♛ *Alice* left *was 33 when she decided to marry Henry. 'Apart from my great happiness in getting married,' Alice wrote later, 'I felt too that it was time I did something useful with my life'*

♛ *Lord William Scott* above *was Henry's closest friend and Alice's older brother. It was through him that Alice and Henry first met*

♛ Below *Henry had other things on his mind in the summer of 1935, but duty came first. Here, he pins a decoration on a scout at a rally held at Balmoral*

Hulton Picture Company

☝Left On 6 June 1935 the Duke of Gloucester unveiled a Silver Jubilee portrait of George V at Australia House in London – just one of his many public engagements. He had recently returned from a seven-month-long tour of Australia. How to combine the roles of Prince of the Royal Family and professional soldier was always a dilemma for Henry and, to his great regret, it was his Army career that suffered

☝ The newly engaged couple below were able to enjoy a few weeks of privacy before a public announcement was made. Henry was based at his regiment's camp in Catterick, Yorkshire, and Alice stayed with friends at Raby Castle. On one of their weekends together the two found time to attend a charity fête in the grounds of Kinmount in Dumfriesshire.

Alice, of course, caught only the odd glimpse of him at these times but they established an easy friendship on his 'bona fide' visits to the Buccleuch home. Although her mother was more formal, the rest of the family treated Harry just like any other of Billy's pals. This was a welcome relief to Harry, whose life was so hidebound with protocol, and one of the main reasons he felt so at home with them. 'To me he was significant only as one of the more regular visitors from among Billy's regimental friends – shy, unassuming and always happy to join in the fun,' Alice recalled later.

Premonition of the future

Alice and Harry continued to meet at various social events over the years. It was not in his nature to advertise his feelings, but she was always aware that he cared for her in a special way. 'I had an instinct that one day we would marry,' she wrote later, 'and perhaps, without ever really admitting it as much to myself, I went to Kenya for the last taste of freedom, before

frequently escaped the routine and tedium of barrack life by slipping up to London. Although expected to stay at Buckingham Palace – where his movements were strictly monitored – on many occasions he stayed with Billy at the Duke of Buccleuch's grand London residence at 2 Grosvenor Place.

These unscheduled forays were a closely guarded secret. Even the Duke and Duchess of Buccleuch were unaware that one of the King's sons was regularly passing the night under their

'*I see a crown and much to do with the Army. You will travel greatly, many long distances*'

A SOOTHSAYER TO ALICE

roof. In fact, the only person entrusted with all the details was the butler, Rowland. With his help the two Cavalry officers were able to plan their London interludes with military precision. Rowland would be waiting when they arrived late in the evening, making sure the coast was clear. After changing out of their uniforms, the two young men would set off for a night out on the town. Rowland would be on hand when they returned for a few snatched hours of sleep, ready to wake them before seven o'clock so they could be on parade by eight.

Hulton Picture Company

abandoning a truly private life for ever.'

That day was heralded when they were both invited to stay with Princess Alice and the Earl of Athlone for Royal Ascot week in 1935. She was then 34 and, as she said herself, 'I had had a very good innings.' Harry was an acutely shy and reserved suitor. There was no question of him wooing her with roses or poetic declarations of undying love. His intentions, however, were no less obvious for being silent. But Alice was determined not to give him any help. He was still very unsure of her feelings when she returned to London after Ascot was over.

Shy Prince Henry might be, but he was also persistent. He persuaded Alice to join him on the long walks he took in Richmond Park with his dogs. And it was there, alone and far from prying eyes, that their romance had its true beginnings.

But they were not as invisible as they believed. Billy, answering the phone at Grosvenor Place, was asked by a reporter for confirmation of rumours linking Lady Alice with Prince Henry. 'First I've heard of it,' Billy replied, pretending to be a footman. And for a while, at least, the hounds were thrown off the scent.

Prince Henry proposes

Towards the end of the summer of 1935 Harry was posted to Catterick again. Alice joined him for a weekend party at Kinmount, the home of a mutual friend in south-west Scotland. It was there, during one of their walks, that Prince Henry asked her to marry him. Characteristically, he did not get down on one knee, but put it to her more as a muttered aside. By now, though, both of them knew that Alice would accept.

👑 *News of the couple's engagement was broadcast to the world on Friday 30 August 1935. The* Daily Mirror's *front-page spread above included such information as 'Lady Alice is shorter than the Duke, who is the tallest of the King's sons.' News of the death in a car crash of Queen Astrid of Belgium was pushed on to page three. Two days later above left the couple were photographed at Balmoral with the King and Queen and Alice's mother, the Duchess of Buccleuch*

WEDDING PRESENTS

The new Duke and Duchess of Gloucester were inundated with wedding presents, and Alice had over 1200 thank-you letters to write. The gifts were all displayed at St James's Palace and the public was charged a fee for admission, which went to charity. Those who went saw the fabulous jewels that Alice had been given by members of her new family, and cabinets crammed with gold and silver plate. More modest gifts included a lace handkerchief and a pretty pair of blue bedroom slippers. Two crofters from Harris in the Outer Hebrides presented the couple with two rolls of Harris tweed, which they took to Buckingham Palace in person *right*. However, like many newlyweds, Alice and Henry also received many ugly objects, as well as things it was hard to find a use for. Perhaps the elephant tusk from the Aga Khan came into this category. These gifts were put into store and brought out only if the person who gave one of them came to visit

👑**Left** *Alice arriving back in London after attending the funeral of her father, the Duke of Buccleuch, in Scotland. His death was not unexpected – he had been suffering from cancer for several years. It was decided to go ahead with the wedding in 14 days' time as planned because the King's health was also very poor, and not likely to improve. His Majesty died, in fact, just over two months later*

BETROTHAL AND MARRIAGE

To be closer to her fiancé, Alice went to stay with Lord and Lady Barnard whose home, Raby Castle, was quite close to the Camp. The couple enjoyed some very happy days together. They went for leisurely drives around the countryside, scoured local antique shops in search of bits and pieces for their future home, and ate in secluded country inns. Because the engagement was still unofficial they were able to enjoy this private and romantic interlude undisturbed.

The Duke of Buccleuch was extremely ill now and both Alice and Harry were worried that their news would exacerbate his condition. But the Duke, who had long guessed something was afoot, reacted philosophically. Knowing how much his daughter had always valued her freedom, however, he asked her if she was quite sure she was equal to the task. Marrying Prince Henry, he reminded her, meant she would automatically become a servant of the country.

The King approves

King George's response was one of unqualified pleasure. 'I must send you a line to say how delighted the Queen and I are that my son Henry is engaged to be married to your third daughter Alice,' he wrote to the Duke. 'When I met you at Lords the other day I should have liked to have mentioned the subject, but there were too many people in the room. I trust you have given your consent. Our families have known each other for so many generations now, that it gives me great pleasure to think that they will be more closely connected still. I have not met your daughter

yet, but hope to do so soon and I am sure I shall find her charming. She will certainly receive a warm welcome from my family.'

On 29 August 1935 the King made the official announcement. Shortly afterwards, Alice and her mother were invited to Balmoral. Alice had always been more at home on horseback than in glittering society and her wardrobe reflected that. Having nothing suitably smart, she had to borrow a silk dress from one of her sisters. The visit did not get off to a smooth start. On

👑**Above** *The Glass Coach (so called because of its large glass windows) carries Alice and her brother Walter to Buckingham Palace. Traditionally, the Glass Coach is used to take the bride and groom to the wedding breakfast. But in this case both ceremony and reception were held in Buckingham Palace. Plans to use Westminster Abbey had been scrapped when the death of Alice's father plunged the entire Scott family into mourning*

👑**Right** *Mrs Thomas of Dalston, London, was determined to get a good view of the wedding procession – so determined that she bagged her front-row seat in Green Park at one o'clock in the morning. She was the first member of the public to turn up*

PRICE ONE SHILLING.

WEDDING NUMBER

THE ILLUSTRATED

LONDON NEWS

AMO

placed next to him to keep him awake.

The wedding was planned for 6 November 1935, in Westminster Abbey. In mid-October Alice received word from Bowhill, the family residence in the Borders, that her father was dying. On 18 October she flew north to be at his side. She arrived to find him already unconscious and the next day he died.

A first reaction was to postpone the wedding. But as the King's health was such that he, too, could die at any time, it was decided to go

'I had an instinct that one day we would marry'

ALICE ON HENRY

ahead as planned. Everybody agreed, however, that a grand wedding would now be inappropriate. It was decided that, instead of the Abbey, the wedding would take place in Buckingham Palace's private chapel. There would be no dignitaries present – invitations were restricted to immediate family and close friends.

The wedding day dawned grey and drizzling. The bride and her brother Walter, who was giving her away, made the short journey from 2 Grosvenor Place to the Palace in the Glass Coach, escorted by 12 mounted police. The route was lined with cheering crowds and Alice, dressed from head to toe in the palest pink, had her first taste of what it was like to be the focus

the first morning, Alice, assuming she would be expected to accompany her fiancé in whatever he was doing, told the King that she was about to go stalking. His Majesty was not pleased. Later Henry explained her mistake. Apparently, ladies at Balmoral were not even allowed to watch the grouse shooting, let alone go stalking.

Back in London, however, she began to spend a lot of time at Buckingham Palace and Alice and her prospective father-in-law began to get to know each other better. He had a habit of dozing off at the dinner table and, as her anecdotes often made him laugh, she was always

The wedding was heavily covered by all the newspapers and some even produced special editions top. The picture above in the Daily Sketch was published on the day of the wedding. The artist had to guess how the scene would look

Right The Duke and his Duchess, looking quite radiant, survey the huge crowd of well-wishers gathered in the Mall outside the gates of Buckingham Palace

ILN/John Frost Historical Newspapers

Popperfoto

♛ *The wedding cake* above *was a gift from J Lyons and Co. Almost seven feet tall, it weighed 156 pounds. The combined coats of arms of the Dukes of Gloucester and Buccleuch adorned the bottom tier*

♛ *Henry and Alice* right *shared a passion for hunting. During their honeymoon at Boughton in Northamptonshire they took the opportunity for a day out with the local Woodland Fytchley Hunt, much to the delight of their fellow riders*

of intense public attention. Prince Henry, supported by the Prince of Wales and the Duke of York, wore the full dress uniform of a major in the 10th Royal Hussars. Alice was attended by eight bridesmaids, two of whom were the little Princesses of York, Elizabeth and Margaret.

After a simple service in the small white-and-gold chapel, which began at 11.30 am and lasted about half an hour, the assembled company sat down to a lavish wedding breakfast. Despite the shadow overhanging the occasion, it was a happy affair. The only hitch – which visibly annoyed the King – occurred when Harry's sword proved too blunt to cut through the thick icing that covered the cake.

The Duke of Kent had been criticized for the extravagance of his recent foreign honeymoon,

so Alice and Harry decided not to go abroad. They spent a few days at Boughton House, Kettering, the Northamptonshire seat of the Dukes of Buccleuch. Afterwards, they stayed with friends in Northern Ireland and did some woodcock shooting. Then, their honeymoon over, the couple travelled to York, where the Duke's regiment was now posted.

Duty called again all too soon. In mid-January Henry and Alice were summoned to Sandringham, to the side of the rapidly failing King. But Henry was sick himself, with influenza, so Alice went alone. She was there when, at five minutes before midnight on 20 January 1936, King George V died and the short, troubled reign of King Edward VIII began.

THE NEWLYWEDS' FIRST HOME

Henry and Alice's first married home was the Royal Pavilion at Aldershot: a large wooden bungalow built for Queen Victoria to stay in whenever she came down for military reviews. Worried about her privacy, she had ordered the gardeners to deposit great mounds of earth in front of the windows to prevent people from being able to see in.

It had an enormous dining-room and drawing-room, a small sitting-room, main bedroom, bathroom and dressing-room, and guest rooms in one wing. Staff quarters and kitchen were down the hill and connected to the house by a lift and passage – which meant that when the food finally arrived on the table it was none too hot! The house was raised about a foot off the ground on wooden piles. On one occasion a rather overweight guest plonked himself down on a chair and one of the legs went straight through the floor

ROYAL RESIDENCE

BARNWELL

In 1938 Henry and Alice decided to buy a country home. They chose Barnwell Manor in Northamptonshire – a 16th-century stone manor house with extensive grounds and farms – which had once belonged to Alice's father. The previous owners had redesigned the interior in a garish manner, and the Gloucesters had to undertake an ambitious redecoration programme to restore the house to its former glory

♛This aerial photograph *above*, taken the year after Henry and Alice bought Barnwell, shows the tennis court set amid the ruins of the Saxon castle that adjoins the house. Stables and farm buildings can be seen in the upper left-hand corner

♛The family stand in ascending order of seniority on Barnwell's impressive oak staircase *left*

♛Alice and her decorators worked tirelessly through the war years, stripping away the fake Chinese and Tudor interiors and replacing them with restrained decorative schemes that were more in keeping with the exterior of the house. By 1942, when this photograph was taken in the sitting-room *above*, some parts of the house had been finished, but the restoration work was still far from complete

♛Alice, Henry, William and his nanny at Barnwell in the summer of 1943 *left*. Alice was in charge of the garden, and wanted to make it the most colourful one in the country. Henry occasionally cut down some bushes there, but he enjoyed working on the farm far more

INTO THE SPOTLIGHT

WHEN ALICE MARRIED HENRY, SHE KNEW THAT SHE WOULD BE EXPECTED TO DEVOTE MORE OF HER LIFE TO PUBLIC SERVICE. BUT NEITHER OF THE GLOUCESTERS WAS PREPARED FOR THE PROFOUND CHANGES WHICH THE ABDICATION WOULD BRING

♛ *When Edward VIII above abdicated, Henry once again became third in line to the throne and Regent Designate until Princess Elizabeth came of age. Right Henry and Alice watch the Royal Scots Greys race for the Sprot Cup. Horse-racing was a shared passion and the two loved going to the races*

DESPITE ALL THE BOWING AND CURTSYING, which she found a little disconcerting at first, Alice took her new status easily in her stride. In fact, her new life was not greatly different to the one she had led before. They entertained friends, continued to hunt a lot and Alice enjoyed watching Harry play polo. On the domestic front a comptroller looked after their finances and equerries organized their daily life; Alice's only responsibility was ordering the meals. Their official duties were still few and far between. Harry, a vague man who hated fuss or ceremony – except when it came to the correct dress or uniform to be worn at official occasions

♛Below *At the Webbe Institute in Bethnal Green. Henry loved children and the National Association of Boys' Clubs was one of his favourite patronages*

– gave his wife no advice on how she was now expected to behave. Not that she needed it. The new Duchess of Gloucester soon won everybody's affection and approval with her confidence and charm.

Edward VIII and Mrs Simpson were now spending a lot of time at Fort Belvedere. Its proximity to the Royal Pavilion made them practically neighbours and every so often the newlyweds were invited over to dinner. Like the rest of the family Prince Henry was deeply worried about the liaison, so these invitations were always accepted with mixed feelings. Despite the Gloucesters' unease, however, Mrs Simpson's consummate skills as a hostess ensured that the occasions were relaxed and enjoyable. The dinner was always excellent, the atmosphere informal, and the evening invariably included a

game of *vingt-et-un* or rummy or the screening of a favourite film. But all was far from well. Edward was much closer to Wallis than he had been to any of his previous companions, and tension over the King's relationship with the American divorcée was building up swiftly.

Edward VIII abdicates

It broke clamorously on 10 December 1936. Together with his brothers, Albert and George, Harry had the sad and unprecedented duty of adding his signature to the Instrument of Abdication. Edward's decision to renounce the throne for the woman he loved thrust the crown on the shy Duke of York and – as Princess Elizabeth was still only ten – promoted Prince Henry to Regent Designate. It was a profoundly unwelcome position because it effectively ended his hopes for a proper career as a soldier. Army life suited Prince Henry down to the ground and he had always looked forward to the day when he would command his own regiment of the Hussars. Now his potential obligations to the new King ruled that out forever.

Despite their changed circumstances the Gloucesters could not move out of the Royal Pavilion until York House, their new grace-and-favour London residence, was ready. Around the same time they decided to buy a home in the country, and in 1938 they finally found it. Part of the Boughton estate until the Duke of Buccleuch sold it in 1912, Barnwell Manor was a delightful 16th-century house with four

⚜Above *The Duke and Duchess finished their Kenyan holiday with a few days in Nairobi and Henry wrote to Queen Mary that he had not seen Alice looking so well for a long time.* Below *In the King's absence, Prince Henry took the salute at the Trooping of the Colour on 8 June 1939, accompanied by the Duke of Kent*

tenanted farms, built near the remains of a Saxon castle. The previous owners, a Captain and Mrs Cooper, had decorated the old manor at great expense and with flamboyant taste. Undoing their excesses was to prove a long and costly business. However, Henry and Alice's efforts were amply repaid in the happiness Barnwell was to bring them.

1937 was a busy year. There was the Coronation of George VI and a consequent increase in the Gloucesters' official duties. Alice was made Commandant of the St John Ambulance

> ## 'I found everyone bowing
> ## and curtsying rather
> ## embarrassing at first'
>
> ### ALICE ON MARRIED LIFE

Association and Brigade, received the Freedom of Edinburgh, became President of the Royal Academy of Music and accepted her first patronages. One of these, 'Invalid Kitchens', was a voluntary food service for elderly invalids started by her godmother, Lady Carmichael; it was a forerunner of Meals on Wheels. Prince Henry accepted the presidency of the Australia Club, formed in 1937 to entertain persons of status connected with the country. After hearing an address he made to the club in 1938, the then Governor-General of Australia was prompted to write to the Prince's private secretary that he wished 'more than I can say' that the Duke

YORK HOUSE

York House, designed by Benjamin Wyatt, was built in the precincts of St James's Palace for George IV's brother, the Duke of York. The Duke of Windsor described it as 'a rambling, antiquated structure, a veritable warren with passages interrupted by unexpected flights of stairs leading to unsymmetrical rooms full of ugly Victorian furniture, brass beds, and discarded portraits of former monarchs'. Henry and Alice were there during the bombing of London. Alice gave a vivid description of the damage. 'A piece of pavement about 2 feet square and 4 inches thick was flung into the "Lady-in-Waiting's room" and landed on the writing-table...Another huge jagged piece of concrete, rather larger than a football, landed in the spare bedroom'

would at some future date come to Australia as Governor-General, if only for a couple of years.

That same year saw Harry writing excitedly to tell his mother that Alice had started a baby. Queen Mary was 'enchanted as you are so devoted to children & it will make all the difference to your & darling Alice's happiness'. Alas, three weeks later, Alice suffered a miscarriage. In the autumn of 1938, possibly as a result of her greatly increased workload, Alice miscarried again. The doctor ordered a complete rest and the Gloucesters decided to take a holiday in Alice's beloved Kenya. They spent most of the trip on safari. Harry, though prepared to rough it a bit, was so used to people doing everything for him that it was the practical Alice who had to take charge when things went awry.

The holiday was exactly what Alice needed. The weeks in Kenya gave her a break from her taxing Royal duties and allowed her to relax in her own way. She did not do any shooting, 'as I don't care for it & do not collect heads,' but occupied herself with her camera and sketch-book. Prince Henry fished, played in polo tournaments and did some shooting, but also spent more time watching and photographing the animals from hides near the waterholes.

On their way back to England they spent one night in Paris with the exiled Windsors. Instead of eating at home the foursome went to a smart restaurant. 'I did not feel in the least chic,

with the red dust of Kenya hardly out of my hair,' Alice recalled later, 'but the Duke and Duchess were more than kind.' The encounter was reported in the English press and as a result the Gloucesters were inundated with disapproving letters. They naturally found this very upsetting and nothing they were ever to do again was to prove as controversial.

The shadow of war

As World War 2 loomed ever closer on the horizon, Prince Henry found himself spending more time than ever with the King. On 28 August 1939 George VI wrote to Queen Mary, 'Harry and George have dined with me nearly every night this week.' On 1 September, Germany invaded Poland with a force of 1.25 million men and two days later Britain formally declared itself at war. Harry was appointed Chief Liaison Officer, British Field Force, and on 14 September he left for a secret destination in France. 'My beloved Alice,' he wrote from General Headquarters the next day. 'I did hate leaving you yesterday so very much that I could hardly keep a straight face, & when I looked

♛ *October 1942: the Duchess inspects the nurses after receiving Liverpool's Red Cross Penny-a-Week Fund contributions below. The fund, dependent on voluntary wage deductions, was begun by Prince Henry to help PoWs and the Red Cross war effort*

Crown Copyright

Chief Liaison Officer, GHQ Home Forces, and in this capacity travelled to meet soldiers all over the United Kingdom.

In April 1941, the Duke and Duchess flew to Belfast, arriving the day after the city's first bombardment. They were greeted by widespread devastation and a moving welcome from the people. The Duke and Duchess lost no time in visiting the wounded in hospital. 'The newly blinded men were the most painful casualties to meet,' Alice wrote later, 'and I was almost overcome with emotion myself when a young man, who had just lost his sight, would not let go when I took his hand.'

A personal happiness was about to illuminate their lives, however. A month later Alice was overjoyed to find she was pregnant again. On 31 May, Queen Mary wrote, 'I was so thrilled and delighted at your good news this morning

round to wave to you, Prater had gone already too far.' Apart from three brief leaves, he was to be away until just before the fall of Dunkirk.

Alice made her contribution to the war effort by travelling around the country visiting First Aid posts set up by the St John Ambulance Association and the WAAF. She was also Colonel-in-Chief of The King's Own Scottish Borderers and the Northamptonshire Regiment and in October she accepted the Presidency of the Hospital Supply Branch of the Red Cross.

A subdued Christmas

It was a grim time for the whole country and the family gathering at Sandringham that Christmas was a reduced and subdued affair. Princess Alice was unable to attend because of a severe cold. Prince Henry, with his brother-in-law Billy as his ADC, was braving enemy bombs to visit British troops all over the north of France. At Barnwell the male servants and employees were conscripted into the forces. Assisted by the few people who were too old to join up, Alice dug up most of the garden – including her lovely flowerbeds – and turned it over to potatoes.

An additional worry was the possibility of a German plot to parachute in and kidnap members of the Royal Family. As a precaution the Gloucesters were assigned a Welsh detective – soon nicknamed 'faithful corgi' – who moved into Barnwell and for the next five years accompanied Alice everywhere.

Prince Henry was determined not to be simply a 'royal ornament' in France. Whenever possible he played an active and often dangerous part. Many testified to his extraordinary capacity for memorizing the order of battle, both British and German. Back in Britain he was appointed

Hulton Picture Company

⚜**Top** *The Duke of Gloucester, the Commander-in-Chief and the Quartermaster General at breakfast at their quarters in France. Prince Henry's plans for a military career had been frustrated by the change in his Royal status, but the war saw him back in the Army as Chief Liaison Officer. At home the Duchess was working equally hard, making use of her connections with the Red Cross and St John Ambulance Brigade to visit wounded Tommies* above *and offer her sympathy, concern and gratitude on behalf of both the King and the nation*

that I nearly fell off my dressing table stool in my excitement!' Two months later she was writing again in her usual thrifty vein, 'Fortnum and Mason are *so expensive* that I think you had better go elsewhere for the cradle.' She also advised Alice to find out exactly what items of the baby's layette could be bought with coupons.

During the final days of the Duchess's pregnancy, her doctor had X-rays taken to help him decide on the best way to deliver the child. These were sent to Prince Henry, who studied them earnestly and even sought the opinion of his commanding officer on several occasions: poor Brigadier Fanshawe was driven to hiding in his bedroom but there was no escaping the anxious father. When the Duke knocked on his door, the Brigadier leapt fully dressed into bed

Windsor on 22 February. The names chosen were William Henry Andrew Frederick. Once again Harry was only granted a brief leave. 'What a pity Harry will miss 3 months of the baby's adorable baby days which one simply loves,' commiserated Queen Mary, 'especially the first one! You cannot think how Papa enjoyed our first baby (that naughty boy!!!) he was always in and out of the nursery.'

Death of the Duke of Kent

On 25 August 1942 Alice and Harry joined George VI and Queen Elizabeth at Balmoral. Halfway through dinner a servant entered and told the King there was a phone call for him. He returned a few minutes later tense and drawn. As Queen Mary was now very old and frail, everyone assumed the phone call was to announce her death. Instead it had brought the devastating news that the young and debonair Duke of Kent had been killed in an aircrash. Harry was deeply affected by the tragic accident. Writing to his mother, he said, 'even now I do not realize I will never see him again. Somehow it all seems a short nightmare instead of reality.'

But his growing family helped him to bear his grief. William was a healthy, active toddler – too active sometimes for his grandmother's peace of mind. 'So William is walking already,' she wrote on 30 November 1942, 'much too soon, don't let him get bandy-legged!' To his parents, however, he was a continual source of pride and joy. In 1943 Alice was reporting that the two-year-old was 'always covered with bruises and scratches as he is very inquisitive and venturesome and will climb under and over and on to everything, usually in a hurry, and then trips over something and takes a crash! But he is very brave and never cries much.'

In 1944 Alice was expecting again, and in

Hulton Picture Company

♔ *Baby Prince William plays happily with a model Spitfire* above, *innocently foreshadowing his tragically early death at the age of 30 in a flying accident*

'*Oh! the joy I felt when I heard you & Alice had got a boy & that your great wish has been fulfilled after all these years!*'

QUEEN MARY

♔ *William's little brother Richard* right *was christened at a private ceremony in Windsor Castle on 20 October 1944, just eight weeks after his birth on 26 August*

and pretended to be asleep. Henry shook him, forcing Fanshawe to try and explain why he was wearing uniform in bed. It must have been a relief to all when, on 18 December 1941, the Duchess of Gloucester was delivered by Caesarean section of a baby boy. Prince Henry, granted a few days compassionate leave, noted with pride that his son 'is supposed to resemble me.' 'Oh! the joy I felt when I heard you & Alice had got a boy,' Queen Mary wrote to Harry the next day, '& that your great wish has been fulfilled after all these years!'

The christening ceremony took place at

Hulton Picture Company

Popperfoto

♛ *The long voyage to Australia with two small children must have been a daunting prospect, but Alice looked as serene as ever when she and the Duke were photographed at the station with the King, Queen and Duchess of Kent* below. *In fact, William and baby Richard effortlessly captured the hearts of the Australian people, and the family look happy and relaxed in the sunshine* above

August, Richard Alexander Walter George was born. Soon the happy mother was writing that his features were perfect 'except his ears which curl up a little bit'. That same year Prince Henry learned that he was to replace Lord Gowrie as Governor-General of Australia.

The Gloucesters left for Australia on 16 December 1944. Anxiety about the voyage due to the continued presence of German submarines off the Irish coast, was not helped by heavy seas and the ship's zig-zagging to avoid a U-

'It was with mixed feelings that we set off for Australia'

ALICE

boat. Then a depth-charge fired by one of the nine escort vessels violently rocked the ship and terrified the children. When, on 18 December, his mother tried to console him by telling him it was his third birthday, William replied miserably, 'I don't want a birthday.' He cheered up, however, when the ship's company presented him with a trolley, a toy car and beautiful pink and white birthday cake.

Down under at last

They finally docked in Sydney on 29 January 1945. At a photo-session at Admiralty House William was kept quiet with an orange – an exotic fruit which, because of rationing, had not come his way before. After lunch the Duke drove the Duchess and their two little boys to their official headquarters in Canberra. The crowds who had gathered along the route welcomed them with cries of 'Good old Scotland!', 'Good Old Henry' and 'Hello Dukie!' This friendly reception was much appreciated by the

THE EVACUEES

While Prince Henry was away in France, Alice was told to expect the arrival of children from war-torn London. In the autumn of 1940 three little evacuees arrived at Barnwell Manor. The two boys lived in the staff quarters of the main house while their sister was placed with the butler's family in their house in the grounds. The children were mainly looked after by the cook and Alice's secretary. The Duchess, however, joined in the cricket matches they all played on the lawn and often read to them before they were tucked up in bed. One morning the homesick trio sneaked out at 4 am with the intention of walking back to London. Fortunately they were heading the wrong way and were soon retrieved. Their explanation was that the country was too boring and they wanted to see more of the air raids and bombs

Hulton Picture Company

Gloucesters, but failed to cushion the shock they received on arriving at Government House.

Alice described Government House in Canberra as 'a large pretentious house just sitting in the middle of nothing'. Inside, the Gloucesters were appalled to find rooms virtually bare of furniture, pictures, light fittings and even bed linen. 'Poor Nannie was aghast at the miserable nurseries awaiting her and the children,' Alice wrote on 19 February. 'No electric kettle, no frigidair, nothing we had asked for!' She also wrote that 'The house seems to be full of silver fish, mice and rats and I am constantly removing enormous spiders and dropping them out of the window.' It was not the most encouraging start to their two-year stay. But the Gloucesters bore the difficulties with fortitude and were to develop a deep affection for both Australia and its people.

♚ Australia gave a warm welcome to the Duke and Duchess below, showing them a spontaneous kindness which helped to offset the sorrow the Gloucesters felt at taking up a position which should have been occupied by Henry's brother, the Duke of Kent, tragically killed in an aircrash two years before

Hulton Picture Company

Family Album
The Gloucesters

Camera Press

Popperfoto

♛The rambling old manor house at Barnwell was a childhood paradise for the young Princes of Gloucester. The age gap between the brothers was less than three years and the two boys were very close. *Above* Home for the holidays: ten-and-a-half-year-old William wheels laughing seven-year-old Richard along the path to their playroom

♛*Left* A large pile of grass-cuttings on the freshly mown lawn provides a source of endless entertainment for two small boys in the summer of 1948. A chubby Prince Richard also appears to have been plundering the flower-beds. Richard and William were too small to remember Barnwell when they returned to England with their parents in 1947 but, for the boys, life was not so very different from Australia and they settled down happily in their home in the rolling Northamptonshire countryside

Hulton Picture Company

✠ *Left* Well wrapped up against the cold, the Duchess and Prince William watch the National Pony Society's 41st Show of Polo and Riding Ponies in 1947, together with the Duke and family friends Lord and Lady Digby at the Roehampton Club in London

♛ *Below left* Prince Richard tranquilly reads a comic as he waits for the train that will take him back to Wellesley House Preparatory School at Broadstairs in Kent after the 1954 summer holidays. Both Princes went to Wellesley House, and then on to Eton and Cambridge

♛ *Below* A rare moment of quiet and intense concentration: Richard, aged nine-and-three-quarters, and William, aged eleven-and-a-half, sit engrossed in a game of chess in the upstairs playroom at Barnwell

Popperfoto

Tom Blau/Camera Press

FAMILY LIFE

Having waited so long before starting a family, their two children were doubly precious to Alice and Henry. They enjoyed William and Richard's childhoods to the full and were determined that the boys, when grown, would look back with many fond memories to times spent at home and on holiday with their parents

♔ The family poses for the camera outside Barnwell Manor *below*. During the 'fifties, when the boys were at school (Wellesley House followed by Eton), the centre of family life was Barnwell. Henry taught them to shoot and play cricket and both Alice and Henry took them out riding as often as possible

♔ Alice enjoyed an idyllic childhood in Edwardian England, just before the golden age of the British aristocracy was ended by World War 1. This photograph *right* was taken in 1908. Alice, six years old, is sitting with a book on her knee. With her is her sister Mary, who was four at the time

♛Henry gave Alice a magnificent diamond tiara and diamond and emerald brooch set *left* as a wedding present. It was displayed in St James's Palace for several weeks after the wedding, together with all the other gifts sent to the happy couple by family, friends and well-wishers

♛*Right* Alice and Henry with their son William on holiday at Devonport, Tasmania, where they spent many happy hours on the beach. Henry was Governor-General of Australia for two years in the mid-1940s, and he and the family retained a special affection for Australia ever after

AP/Topham

♛*Below* William and his father in July 1943. Born six years after his parents' marriage, when Alice was 40, William was a much-wanted child who inherited his father's fearlessness in full measure. Both Alice and Henry were devastated when his life was cut short by an accident during an air race in 1972

Hulton Picture Company

'Nature has endowed this country with so much that the old country lacks...'

ALICE ON AUSTRALIA

TWIN TRAGEDIES

FROM AUSTRALIA, THE GLOUCESTERS RETURNED HOME TO A LIFE THAT WAS BUSIER THAN EVER. ALICE TREASURED THE RARE MOMENTS WITH HER FAMILY, SENSING, PERHAPS, THAT THEIR TIME TOGETHER WAS RUNNING OUT

PRINCE HENRY WAS NOW AN EXPERIENCED front-line Royal, but he still found formal occasions an ordeal and, of course, his new position required him to play a leading role in State ceremonies. Fortunately, his dislike of pomposity, linked with a boyish sense of humour, meant that as far as he was concerned, the occasional mishap was an event which helped lighten the proceedings. On one occasion, the Duke was in the middle of knighting a distinguished old gentleman. While the man was kneeling with his back to the assembled company, a mouse dashed behind him with a cat hard on its heels. A ripple of giggles ran through the crowd and the poor man 'blushed scarlet, obviously thinking his trousers must have split or something'.

Star of the show

William and Richard were to prove a great asset to the Duke and Duchess in their work. Australians love children and the atmosphere was always more relaxed when they were around. So much so, in fact, that when four Office of Work employees disappeared while hanging pictures for the Royal couple, Alice discovered them in a corridor turning somersaults with William! The little boy was always the star of the show wherever he went. *The Australian Woman's Weekly* proclaimed him 'William the Conqueror, the travelling salesman of Britain,' saying 'He had broken the ice at many official functions, for formality vanishes when a small boy enlivens the proceedings.'

There were worries too, though. Prams and the childrens' hats had to be netted against the ever-present flies, and the presence of poisonous snakes made it too dangerous for William and his friends to play in the gardens. Fortunately this last problem was solved when the family acquired an Australian terrier who proved to be expert at getting rid of snakes.

Prince Henry had determined to visit the capital of every state in the country within the first six months of his tenure and by VE Day, in May 1945, he had almost succeeded. Everywhere they went the Gloucesters were warmed, not only by welcoming crowds, but by many individual acts of kindness and generosity.

Hulton Picture Company

Camera Press

♔*Always keen on recording the environment surrounding her, Alice enjoyed taking photographs left as well as painting; she once won a Diploma of Honour in a photography competition*

♔Left *Celebrating the Prince's 46th birthday with a swim at Palm Beach, New South Wales. By this time the couple's private life had settled into a familiar routine. Government House had become more comfortable and they found time for riding, tennis and family picnics as well as swimming. Evenings at home were cosy, with the Duke and Duchess playing paper games or screening movies.*

The official side of their second year in Australia consisted largely of touring country areas and visiting agricultural shows. During the two years they spent in that country, they covered 76,000 miles in Endeavour, *their specially equipped aircraft. In 1947, Henry and Alice returned home to England where, again, official engagements were the order of the day: in March they inspected the extensive flood damage at the Earith Gap in the banks of the River Ouse in Cambridgeshire above*

arrived back on 19 November, the eve of the wedding of Princess Elizabeth and Prince Philip. The magnificent ceremony was held in Westminster Abbey and little William was one of the pages. In February 1948 they were off again, this time to Ceylon to open the Dominion Parliament on behalf of the King. The Duke and Duchess made an overnight stop at Habbaniya – a stay which proved highly embarrassing for the RAF captain assigned to look after them. As he was getting ready to see them off, he discovered that part of his uniform had been stolen. Rushing outside, the hapless officer was just in time to see the thief disappearing down the street clutching his booty. He fired warning shots after him but unfortunately failed to recapture his trousers.

The Gloucesters were to undertake a great many official trips in the years to come. In 1950 they visited Kenya again for the Golden Jubilee of Nairobi, creating the town a city, and to mark the occasion they brought with them a splendid mace. It was a particularly pleasurable trip and

Henry also made the first-ever visit by a Governor-General to the island of Norfolk, situated 1000 miles out in the Pacific Ocean. The isolation of the tiny sliver of land – only six miles long – was awesome. The island's 800 inhabitants were all descendants of the nine mutineers of the *Bounty* and their Tahitian wives, and the official lunch given in the Gloucesters' honour took the form of a picnic attended by the entire population. It was a unique occasion and one of the most memorable of their Australian experiences.

Henry's tenure ended in 1947. King George VI's decision to visit South Africa with his wife and daughters meant that the Regent Designate had to stand in for him at home. Despite initial inconveniences and the various health problems that had beset all of them, the Gloucesters were sad to leave. In her farewell message, Alice expressed the affection and esteem they they had come to feel for both Australia and the big-hearted Australian people.

Home again

On their return to England they found Barnwell's grounds an overgrown tangle of weeds and York House seriously damaged by the bombing. It was to take much time and effort before everything was put right. However, by the time Queen Mary paid a visit to Northamptonshire in August 1947, considerable progress had been made. 'I enjoyed seeing all the improvements you have made at Barnwell,' she wrote to Harry afterwards, 'for I must confess that when I last saw the place in 1939 I had no idea that you would be able to transform it into a really charming and comfortable home.'

In the autumn of that same year the Duke and Duchess paid a state visit to Malta. They

♛ *The Gloucesters always made a point of doing things together as a family, and they brought their children up with as little fuss and formality as possible. In January 1948 they took six-year-old William (on the left in front) to Bertram Mills's Circus at Olympia in London* top. *Also part of the group were Henry's aide-de-camp, Colonel Howard Kerr, and his son*

♛ *As Richard poses for a photograph at the wedding of the Earl of Dalkeith and Jane McNeill in 1953, his mother steps forward to tidy his hair* above

gave the Duke and Duchess a much-appreciated opportunity to renew acquaintance with relatives and old friends. The day of the Charter ceremony coincided with Harry's 50th birthday, and the crowds responded with a hearty rendering of 'Happy Birthday'.

That autumn William started boarding school at Wellesley House, Broadstairs. Richard followed him and both subsequently passed their common entrance exams into Eton. During school holidays Henry was enthusiastic about teaching his sons to shoot and happily participated in activities such as riding, croquet, picnics and cricket. He left Alice, however, to keep them amused indoors and read them stories. In between public obligations, the two

THE SOCIAL ROUND

In the course of their work the Gloucesters attended hundreds of official dinners. An unusual problem once arose when Alice was placed next to de Gaulle at a banquet given by Sir Edmund and Lady Stockdale. First he complimented her on the beauty of her daughter, then asked how she had enjoyed her recent visit to the chateaux of the Loire. From these puzzling remarks she realized that the short-sighted General thought she was the hostess. Alice tactfully remained Lady Stockdale for the rest of the evening.

Winston Churchill *above* was always delighted to find himself placed next to the Duchess because it meant a constant supply of champagne. A teetotaller herself, Alice allowed her glass to be continually refilled throughout the meal for Winston's benefit

grown-ups enjoyed country life. While Harry concentrated on the farm, Alice kept an eye on the garden. They also enjoyed scouring antique shops for the miniature elephants, sporting prints and old books he collected.

The King had undergone a major operation for lung cancer in October 1951. He failed to make a proper recovery and his death on 6 February 1952 stunned and saddened the nation. The loss was particularly painful to Prince Henry, who was devoted to his brother and relied greatly on his good advice.

Death of a Queen

The Gloucesters were prevented from joining the family at Sandringham that Christmas as Richard had German measles. Queen Mary wrote to tell Harry how disappointed she was at not seeing him. 'Darling Mama,' Prince Henry replied on 28 January 1953, 'I have just heard from Lilibet that you leave Sandringham tomorrow, which is very sad for us, as we shall just miss seeing you there.' He went on to say he hoped she was getting out and about more, ending 'Best love from your most devoted boy Harry.' It was the last letter he ever wrote to her and concluded a correspondence that had continued uninterrupted for almost 50 years. On 24 March, 86-year-old Queen Mary died and the Royal Family were plunged into mourning again.

♛ *On the morning of the Coronation of Elizabeth II in June 1953, the Gloucester family rose at 5 am to get ready. William and Richard were dressed in new kilts and coats, and Alice looked most impressive in her stately robes above. After the ceremony Henry rode in the procession and Alice and the boys shared a carriage with Mary, the Princess Royal. It was pouring with rain and the two boys found the long drive very tedious. But Mary kept everyone entertained by recounting anecdotes about amusing mishaps she recalled happening on grand occasions of the past*

♛ *Henry and Alice visited William at Eton for the St Andrew's Day celebrations in 1956 right*

Hulton

The Coronation in June helped to lift everyone's spirits. Then Henry and Alice plunged once more into their travels. In August 1957 Prince Henry represented Queen Elizabeth II at Malaya's independence celebrations. Ports of call during the following years included Africa, Cyprus, Greece, Turkey, Malta, Kenya, Jordan and Palestine. Between tours, life in England was as busy as ever. There was the usual round of official engagements and, in June 1962, Henry and Alice gave a magnificent ball at Barnwell to celebrate William's coming of age. The Queen came down in her own train and kindly put up several of the guests overnight.

The first blow

In 1965, while preparations were being made for a five-week tour of Australia, the Gloucesters travelled to London to attend Winston Churchill's funeral. It was on the drive back to Barnwell that they were involved in the car crash from which Prince Henry never fully recovered.

The Duke's health had begun to fail and it seemed that his childhood weakness of the legs had returned to plague him. Long walks and shooting were a thing of the past. His doctors had also told him to give up driving which, as it was his sole remaining pleasure, he hated to do. Although he was clearly very tired that morning,

Henry and Alice pose for a Silver Wedding anniversary photo in the doorway of Barnwell Manor, 6 November 1960 left

The years of the late 1950s and early 1960s saw the Duke and Duchess constantly on the move. In 1959 they visited Kano in Nigeria, where the Emir read a welcoming address to them at his gaily decorated mud palace below. Then in 1961 Henry, as President of the Commonweath War Graves Commission, travelled to Greece and Turkey to tour military cemeteries. Alice accompanied him on his visit, which included a donkey ride to the ruins of a mountain-top temple on the island of Rhodes left

Hulton Picture Company

Alice was unable to dissuade him from taking the wheel. They had almost made it safely home when the Rolls suddenly swerved over a ditch and rolled three times before landing in a cabbage field. Henry was thrown into some brambles and escaped seemingly unhurt, though it is possible that he had suffered the first of a series of strokes which would eventually confine him to a wheelchair and deprive him of almost all speech and understanding. The chauffeur, who was sitting in the back, suffered cracked ribs and the Duchess was discovered unconscious and bleeding heavily. By lucky chance, a coach carrying a team of miners belonging to the St John Ambulance Brigade was

Alice suffered deep facial wounds, a broken arm and nose and a cracked knee when the Rolls she and Henry were travelling in overturned on the way back from Churchill's funeral. Luckily they were rescued by some miners. Alice remembers nothing until she came round to find herself being gently lifted by four strong arms: 'I am sure no one could have done better than they in saving my life and preventing me from suffocating from the blood pouring down my throat from my nose,' she said. She was still looking badly bruised when she left Bedford Hospital several days later right

Topham

Evening Standard

Queen's cousin killed
—plane crashes and
explodes in air race

PRINCE WILLIAM DIES IN CRASH

WILLIAM

The life of William Henry Andrew Frederick, Henry and Alice's eldest son, was brought to a tragically early end on 28 August 1972, when the plane he was flying in crashed. William read history at Magdalene College, Cambridge, and it was there that he learned to fly. After university he studied at Stanford University in California for a year then, back home, joined a merchant bank in the city for six months. In 1965 he joined the Commonwealth Relations Office and was appointed Third Secretary at the British High Commission in Lagos. Three years later he was posted to Tokyo; he travelled there in a Piper Comanche aircraft with co-pilot Vyrell Mitchell, who was to be killed, along with Richard, four years later. In 1970, his father's ill health forced him to give up his career in diplomacy to look after Barnwell and take on some public duties. Popular with both men and women, 30-year-old Prince William was greatly mourned

'He was always such a restless, active person that I have often wondered if he had some premonition that his life was destined to be short'

ALICE ON WILLIAM

👑 *Henry's funeral. Alice is flanked by her only surviving son, Richard, and her daughter-in-law Birgitte right; the flower-bedecked coffin is carried down the steps of St George's Chapel, Windsor far right. Henry's last years had been difficult, and his death must have come as a welcome relief for both himself and his family, but it was a tremendous blow for Alice, who was still grieving for William*

Camera Press

👑**Above** *the Royal Family lines up at the wedding of Richard and Birgitte van Deurs, the daughter of a Danish lawyer, on 8 July 1972. The couple met at a tea party on Richard's second day at Cambridge. He was studying architecture at Magdalene College and she, English at a local language school. After university, Richard and two partners set up an architectural practice in London, but after his father's death in 1974 he was forced to give up his career in order to assume the title of Duke of Gloucester and the management of the estate of Barnwell. He has taken on the role efficiently, and is patron of many organizations, including ASH (Action for Smoking and Health); his first speech in the House of Lords was aimed at the tobacco industry. The couple, who have three children – Alexander, born in 1974; Davina, born in 1977; and Rose, born in 1980 – live at Barnwell and also have an apartment at Kensington Palace*

following behind them, and they effected a rescue.

Despite their near-catastrophe, the Gloucesters arrived in Australia only one week later than planned. Their tour, which was supposed to be 'leisurely and informal', was nonetheless quite rigorous, and Henry probably suffered another stroke during the Anzac Day ceremony on 25 April. His last overseas mission was to Malaysia in January 1966, after which he needed constant nursing: by 1968 he was almost paralyzed.

When Prince William returned home in 1970 to take up his father's duties, Alice felt she hardly knew the restless, active man her beloved son had become. Alice looked forward to spending time with William, now that the family were together again, but it was not to be. Prince Henry's nurse was only present during the day, so when William arrived home in the evenings, Alice could not leave her husband. Just two years later, William entered an air race in Staffordshire. Alice was at Barnwell when she was told that his plane had crashed and her beloved eldest son was dead.

A month before William's death, Richard married the Danish Birgitte van Deurs. Although

47

'...all around are reminders of past happiness'

ALICE AT BARNWELL

♛**Below** *Alice at her beloved Barnwell. The Princess has a small suite at Kensington Palace, where she usually lives during the week, but weekends are spent in the country with Richard and his family. She welcomes the peace and contentment of life at the family estate, and realizes that, after a long and industrious life, she is finally free to enjoy it with a clear conscience*

unable to comprehend what was happening, it was hoped the Duke sensed the joyfulness of the occasion. He had always been a fond and indulgent father, only occasionally losing his temper when the boys misbehaved.

On 10 June 1974, two years after the death of his eldest son, Prince Henry lost his slender grip on life. He was buried at Frogmore close to two people he had loved dearly: his brother, the Duke of Windsor; and his son William. Henry had been a dutiful Prince, accepting his Royal tasks willingly but without great enthusiasm. He once joked, during a conversation about Princess Marie Louise's memoirs, 'I am thinking of writing my own [memoirs]. And do you know what I shall call them? *Forty Years of Boredom.*'

With the death of her husband and son, no more annual holidays in Scotland and finding herself too old now to ride, Alice's life seemed suddenly empty of much that had brought her

happiness. She considered retiring to Barnwell, to enjoy her gardens and possibly take up painting again. But as the weeks passed, feeling began to return. The Duchess remembered the many public engagements she had promised to fulfil, and the idea of cloistering herself in the country receded. At the age of 73, Princess Alice, as she was now known, squared her shoulders and took up her Royal responsibilities again.

A wholehearted life

Having travelled so much during her life, Alice was now well content to work at home. She did, however, make a third visit to Australia to visit Richard and Birgitte, taking Alexander and Davina, her adored grandchildren, with her. Early in 1981 she also returned to Kenya, making a special trip to Deloraine. Here she found the gardens as lovely as ever, with shrubs she had helped to plant 50 years earlier a blaze of riotous colour. Then, at the age of 81, Alice published her memoirs, which were well received.

The pledge made to God long ago in the turbulent waters off the Cumberland shore had been honoured. She had made use of her life as she promised, dedicating it wholeheartedly to the service of King and Country.

G. Mathews/Camera Press